Skylines

Also by Elizabeth Witts

Cobwebs and Catastrophes
Sundials and Safaris

Skylines

Poems 2013-2014

Elizabeth Witts

Matador
9 Priory Business Park,
Wistow Road, Kibworth Beauchamp,
Leicestershire. LE8 0RX
Tel: (+44) 116 279 2299
Fax: (+44) 116 279 2277
Email: books@troubador.co.uk
Web: www.troubador.co.uk/matador

ISBN 978 1784620 837

British Library Cataloguing in Publication Data.
A catalogue record for this book is available from the British Library.

Typeset in 11pt Garamond by Troubador Publishing Ltd, Leicester, UK
Printed and bound in the UK by TJ International, Padstow, Cornwall

Matador is an imprint of Troubador Publishing Ltd

To my godsons Stephen and Nigel

CONTENTS

IN THE COUNTRY

THE COTSWOLDS MEET THE SKY

The square tower
of Stow Church stands out
on the horizon. A kestrel
flies above the yellow
fields of rape, while overhead
the larks are singing.

Wild flowers and nettles
grow by the grey stone walls,
and in the young grass
the shorn sheep
are calling to their lambs.

A blue and white sign reads
Unsuitable for motors
and there, beyond the lane,
sleeps the rust-red roof
of a deserted barn.

From There to Here

I often look at the sheep
grazing in the fields

as it helps me remember
why I'm here.

My ancestors from Holland
migrated to England

because of the wool
and made a livelihood

as fustian makers,
unlike their relations

John and Cornelius de Witt
who were lynched

at the Hague, this is true,
in Sixteen Seventy Two.

A Favourite Place

I stand beside this five-barred gate
on dark days when I want to scream
against the vagaries of fate –
my only witnesses are sheep.
This lane was once a Roman road
with war-like legions marching by,
now it's a lonely track that goes
across the hills, straight as a die.

A hawthorn tree grows by the wall,
finches fly out on golden wings,
down in the woods a pheasant calls,
above my head a skylark sings.
The open fields release my tears
and pent-up anger disappears.

IN THE RAIN

This summer, in the pouring rain,
I walk along a country lane,

cow parsley overshadows me
and stinging nettles brush my feet,

blue scabius and yellow vetch
hide in the grasses, dripping wet,

and snails come out into the road
with spiral shells of brown and gold,

tough brambles climb the grey stone walls
and still the drenching raindrops fall.

IN THE SUN

The sun comes out, the rain has passed,
I'm standing barefoot on the grass,

the wind is rustling through the trees,
I take deep breaths and do Tai Chi.

The larks fly up into the sky,
wood pigeons call, the stream runs by,

wild strawberries grow sweet and red,
dog-roses sway and bow their heads.

I hear the church clock striking eight,
it's breakfast time, it's getting late.

An English Summer

Raspberries, strawberries, blueberries, gooseberries,
spoonfuls of sugar and lashings of cream,

cucumber sandwiches, white linen tablecloths,
glasses of iced lemon tea – the summer is here.

Forked flashes of lightning, deep rumbles of thunder,
the milk's going off and the midges are biting,

then torrents of rain sweep the picnics away –
the weather has broken, the summer has ended.

CROQUET

First, take the mallets and the balls,
the red and yellow, black and blue,
then stick the white hoops in the lawn
and show us all what you can do.

Beware the patches in the grass
where badgers scuffed around last night,
watch out for mole-hills as you pass,
go straight ahead, not left or right.

Just hit your ball through narrow hoops
and if you miss don't be downcast,
but keep your temper as you lose –
you might enjoy the game at last!

THE PEACOCK BUTTERFLY

Why do you wear those sapphire rings?

I try to frighten you away,
the circles on my outstretched wings
will keep my enemies at bay.

But, oh! I love your glimmering,
your gold and purple eyes. Please stay!

THE LILAC-BREASTED ROLLERS

You'll find a pair or two
in the Edinburgh Zoo

acrobatic showmen
sub-Saharan rollers

diving from a height
rocking as they fly

birds of flashing colours
lilac green and turquoise

their bright exotic feathers
remind me now of Kenya

with the hot sun beating
on cool acacia trees.

Travelling In

Forget about that pilgrimage to Rome,
stay in this country, walk the labyrinth
up on St. Catherine's Hill. Follow the path
of chalk cut through the turf, it winds around
forwards, backwards, sideways, inwards.

Get used to feeling lost, let go and trust
the patterns of the maze, and when you find
the centre, be yourself, and stand in peace.
Then face about again, retrace your steps,
and come back safely to the outside world.

FROM OUTER SPACE

Today it stops me in my tracks,
this heavy object, cold and black,
a rounded shape without a crack,

the Wold Cottage meteorite,
a lump of chondrite, dark as night.
It fell from a tremendous height

over two hundred years ago.
Tate Britain has it now on loan,
the caption says: "Artist not known",

and many visitors are led
to see this traveller, stone dead,
about the size of a human head.

I stand uneasy in its thrall,
feeling terrestrial and small,
wondering where the next will fall.

THE ROLLRIGHT STONES

I find them at last
in an Oxfordshire field
a circle of stones
like stumps of trees

for thousands of years
they've been standing around
close to each other
feet in the ground

ungainly shapes
all covered in lichen
the King's Men they're called
no-one can count them

they wait in the rain
with their limestone King
and Whispering Knights
inviting me in

to an ancient space
where the grass is green
and ghostly figures
march unseen.

In the City

LONDON MEETS THE SKY

The high horizons here
are stiff with aerials,
flag poles and union flags,
pinnacles and spires.
Among them falcons hover,
seagulls fly, and the tall arms
of high-rise cranes break
through the skyline.

The summit of the Shard
is hidden by low-lying clouds.
Window-cleaners move
like mountaineers.
Below them are the swaying
crowns of leafy planes,
and the homespun rows
of terracotta chimney pots.

MIRACLE AT VAUXHALL CROSS

16 January 2013

This morning, in the blinding mist,
a helicopter has got lost,

it tangles with a high-rise crane
then hits the ground engulfed in flames.

Sadly here two people die,
the pilot and a passer-by;

but all the rush-hour trains are spared
annihilation from the air.

THE STORM

It sweeps through London in the night,
this superstorm they call St. Jude,
and hits the Cabinet Office where
a crane collapses on the roof.

The wind is travelling fast and wild
uprooting trees while people sleep,
torrents of rain are streaming down,
leaves and branches block the streets.

Next night the sky is bright once more,
Orion's striding through the stars,
London's dust has been blown away,
the atmosphere is clear as glass.

On the Bridge

The statue of a noble lion,
finely made of white Coade stone,

is high above me as I pass
over to Westminster by bus.

He stands there gazing at the sky
looking up with sightless eyes,

a lion with a great rough mane
dreaming of his Red Lion days

outside a Lambeth brewery.
He says to me, it soon will be

time for a moment of good cheer,
time to enjoy a pint of beer.

PALACES

North of Lambeth Bridge
two palaces of power,
political and spiritual,
confront one another.

To the west is Westminster,
where Gothic pinnacles
of Yorkshire stone
stand out against the clouds,

while to the east is Lambeth,
where Tudor chimney stacks
of deep red brick
rise smokeless to the sky.

Between them flows the Thames
where cormorants still fish
and barges carry their cargoes
downstream and out to sea.

St. Mary Lambeth

Around the mossy tombstones
see them grow
all aglow –
yellow aconites.

Consider the crocuses –
a brief glimpse
of bishops
purple and upright.

Snowdrops push up through the grass –
spring at last
watch them dance
delight in the white.

St. Stephen Rochester Row

A golden cockerel is standing high
above the cross for all the world to see,

a metal rod runs down the steeple's side,
deflecting danger when the lightning strikes,

God's finger reaches out to touch and heal
the faithful people as they pray for peace.

The bells are ringing, earth and heaven meet.

St. Faith's Chapel

Open a heavy
wooden door
inside the Abbey,

enter the stillness
of the silence
that fills the Chapel.

Painted in colours
on the wall
she stands serene,

the virgin martyr,
as a monk in black
kneels at her feet.

Look up at her,
she heals the weary,
teaches to pray.

Restlessness,
despair and doubt
will fall away.

St. Stephen Walbrook

The spire is fragile, joyful, intricate,
and rises up among high buildings where
bright walls of glass reflect the summer sky.
The garden's leafy stillness leads into
the music of the church. Beneath the dome
is set the massive stone of Henry Moore's
great altar in the round.   Here too is found

the antique telephone Chad Varah used
for the Samaritans.   Peter the priest,
resplendent in his cope, preaches today
at choral evensong: "Do not be blind
to the light!" The sun streams in and rests
on Patrick Heron's kneeler, changing it
into a vibrant ring of prayer and praise.

DIAMOND JUBILEE

Through the rain a peal of bells
is ringing out above the Thames

a belfry barge leads a flotilla
in the pageant down the river

flags are flying for Her Majesty
bells are ringing to God's glory

the wind is cold but people cheer
a Queen who's reigned for sixty years.

The London Olympics

The opening night brings a surprise,
the Queen comes flying from the skies,

helicopters circle round
forestalling danger on the ground,

athletes set the games on fire,
running faster, jumping higher,

and squirrels hide their nuts away
in sand where volley-ball is played.

Spectators cheer on Team GB
delighted with each victory,

and every day the TV news
praises those who win and lose,

while Volunteers excel themselves
celebrating Twenty Twelve.

LONDON'S COLOURS

I venture out to Red Lion Square
and have a drink in Orange Street,
I double back to Lemonwell Drive
and leave Green Dragon Lane in peace.

I sail around Blue Anchor Yard
and climb up Violet Hill, it's steep,
then canter home to White Horse Road
and count the rainbows in my sleep.

IN KEW GARDENS

KEW GARDENS MEETS THE SKY

A tall Pagoda in the Chinese style
creates an air of mystery and calm,

the Palm House, with its rounded roof of glass,
invites the sun to shine on sheltered plants,

the Giant Sequoia reaches up and tries
to touch the clouds as they go drifting by.

It's peaceful where the Gardens meet the sky.

REVISITING KEW

When the sun strikes the glasshouse
in the Secluded Garden

and the doors are half-open,
I feel a light wind blowing,

a shifting wind that carries
the scent of winter jasmine,

and I start to remember
the walks we went together

trying to find an answer
to the pain of your cancer.

THE ROSE GARDEN AT KEW

This morning, as the sun comes out,
the wind is blowing from the south,
caressing my reluctant soul,
easing the pains of growing old.
The roses dazzle and delight:
a *Lichfield Angel*, cool and white,
Young Lycidas, deep pink and hot,
the fragrant *Lady of Shalott*.

An angel passes by and brings
a sense of peace on feathered wings,
John Milton's spirit lives on here,
Tennyson haunts the summer air,
angel and poets all conspire
to give a blessing to this hour.

THE CHINESE NETTLE TREE

The leaves are parchment pale,
pointed, delicate.

Here in the sun they float
like particles of gold,

shining, innocent,
ready to fall. But then,

like nettles, will they sting?
Breathless, glittering,

they wait for the autumn gales
to sweep them away.

FAMILY AND FRIENDS

SPARKLING OR STILL?

Sparkling water I maintain
is like a glass of good champagne,
bubbling, fizzing, helping me
to live life with hilarity.

Still water tranquil, cool and clear
is like a glass of mountain air,
I drink it too from time to time
finding calm and peace of mind.

Beside me now two bottles stand
waiting for my outstretched hand,
each of them will quench my thirst,
but which one shall I pick up first?

Briefly, I will stop and think
before I have that vital drink.

The PNEU School

I play the piano and the triangle
at boarding school in war-time Worcestershire,
the Vicar comes to teach geology
and reads us many awe-inspiring tales
from Plutarch's Lives, and so we learn about
the famous Alexander and his steed
Bucephalus, the horse with one blue eye.

We never travel very far because
of petrol rationing, but go for drives
with Silvertail in the small pony trap.
The wireless gives us all the latest news
and tells us when the Russians reach Berlin,
then if it's fine we walk the Malvern Hills
and keep on waiting for the war to end.

BARREN

It's strange this pain
of childlessness
of uselessness

the mark of shame
an empty womb
that bears no fruit

a pain that stays
sharp as a knife
throughout my life

day after day
until I'm gone
and leave no son.

Apple Pie Bed

The school day has ended,
it's time to go to bed.

My feet meet a barrier
of sheets folded back here,

I can't get inside them,
there's nowhere to hide from

the other girls' laughter,
the whispers after dark.

There's no-one to talk to
and nowhere to walk to,

I'll never get to sleep
entangled in these sheets.

WELLINGTONIAS

Children relax and swing
on the lower branches, listening

to the wind and the bird song
as the tall trees mark the way along

a winding drive, the narrow lane
beyond that five-bar gate.

The soft, chunky bark will
tear off in small hands until

the trunks are smooth as stone.
These redwoods stand alone,

far from the Sierras of the West.

VILLAGE CRICKET

Sixes are falling
into the far allotments.
It's almost tea-time.

The tall spectator
sitting in a folding chair,
wearing a sun hat,

reads the newspapers.
An ex-hostage from Beirut
with his grandchildren.

Mock Orange

Between the lilac tree and laurel hedge
this shrub has flowers with a heavy scent

and pale white petals, welcoming the bees.
A gust of wind has caught the soft green leaves

that brush against me walking up the drive.
They give me a caress as I pass by.

I hesitate, and hold my breath. I hear
my Mother's voice, unheard for many years,

calling to me from the open door,
the Syringa's out, and I breathe once more.

At the End

that afternoon a swan
flew over the house

and a door swung in my face
at the hospital

my Father was reliving
the pain of two World Wars

my Mother stayed with him
for the last time

he died that night
a brave soldier at rest

ALZHEIMER'S

Sitting by the window
with the sun streaming in,
my aunt doesn't speak
in her long, bright room.

I play a nursery rhyme
on the grand piano:
baa, baa, black sheep,
have you any wool?

and then from the sofa
I hear a gentle whistle
keeping time with me,
perfectly in tune,

so I go on singing
from the children's book:
yes sir, yes sir,
three bags full.

NOT QUITE OKAY

(1908-2010)

I found four
robins' nests
on the way to the village.
Father said: *She must
learn Shakespeare!*

Alas for me, I fell
into a misery.
Mademoiselle said:
*Vous êtes extrêmement
timide, Beatrice.*

My teacher on the
Blüthner grand piano
said: *I can't understand
why you won't work,
you've got it all there.*

They must have thought
I was not quite okay.
My friend Daphne said:
*You must eat Beatrice,
or you will die!*

I got wafted away
to this rather special
hospital. One of the
nurses said: *Oh, Beatrice,
you could have a lovely life!*

The Portrait

The canvas has been slashed
twice above the head.
She wears a white satin gown
with bare shoulders,

and sits before
a mediaeval tapestry
showing a stag and doe
in a beautiful forest.

Why has this picture,
painted in the fifties,
aroused such antagonism
half a century on?

It goes viral on the internet:
an English rose princess,
an anachronism, a mad girl
in her mad wonderland.

The canvas is repaired,
but the painting fails
to sell at auction,
this latter-day pre-Raphaelite.

THE RED SCARF

The next time we meet
she's wearing it,
the long red scarf

I knitted for her,
sixty stitches to a row
two plain, two purl.

She loves bright colours
and this present
is a lucky guess,

unlike that necklace
the unread book of poems
the wrong-sized gloves.

Today the scarf matches
her scarlet coat
and we have tea together.

HOUSEWORK

Specks of fine dust are falling
like powder, soft and grey.

I take a yellow duster
and sweep them all away,

knowing in my heart of hearts
that they'll be back next day.

At Home

My home is where I feel quite free
to come and go, and be.

I throw the windows open wide
and let fresh air inside.

My friends keep asking me to stay –
it's never quite the same,

they say: *just make yourself at home,*
and wait for me to come.

But if I find their windows shut,
I fling them wide at once

and then I hear outraged remarks
about the sudden draughts.

BARREN

It's strange this pain
of childlessness
of uselessness

the mark of shame
an empty womb
that bears no fruit

a pain that stays
sharp as a knife
throughout my life

day after day
until I'm gone
and leave no son.

REVERIE

a wooden plank
drifts down the Thames
a railway sleeper
or a diving board
half-hidden as
it floats away
towards the sea
out of my sight

taking my dreams
on a slow ride
to deep waters
and far strands
where the poems
start to sing

On the Go

My mind's a traffic island
watching cars go round

my heart's a Morris Minor
making antique sounds

my hands are windscreen wipers
sweeping up and down

my feet are Boris bikers
whistling into town

my spirit is a glider
sailing through the clouds

my life's a racing driver
playing to the crowds.

FOURSCORE YEARS

Food rationing, and rumours of the war,
swimming in the chilly River Teme,
learning to read and write at home before

long days at school and university,
punting on the Cherwell in the spring,
looking for work inside the BBC,

a time of stop-watches and hammering
of typewriters. Then comes a chance to go
on holiday around the world and dip

into the waters of New Zealand's coast,
travelling on to see the USA,
driving, gliding, going with the flow.

The busy decades quickly pass and fade,
the church's ancient voice can still be heard
teaching people of the need to pray.

Depression comes with sudden loss of work,
a time to brush up on theology,
to touch the keyboard of a clavichord,

to paint in watercolours by the sea,
to write new poems with the words well-tuned,
until the precious final years are free

to watch the peacocks in the sun at Kew,
to grieve for all the loving friends who've died,
to swim refreshed around the local pool,

single, childless, British, and baptized
into a life of sadness and delight.

MY NAMES

Elizabeth

Iz

Liz

Lizzy

Fizzy Izzy

Miss Witts

Wittsy

Beth

Elisabeth

Carissima Lisi

Isleton

the

Bisleton

the

Pie